ISBN 978-1-4950-7335-9

HAL•LEONARD®

7777 W. BLUEMOUND RD. P.O. BOX 13819 MILWAUKEE, WI 53213

Visit Hal Leonard Online at
www.halleonard.com

T0019642

THEME FROM CLOSE ENCOUNTERS OF THE THIRD KIND

By JOHN WILLIAMS

Moderately

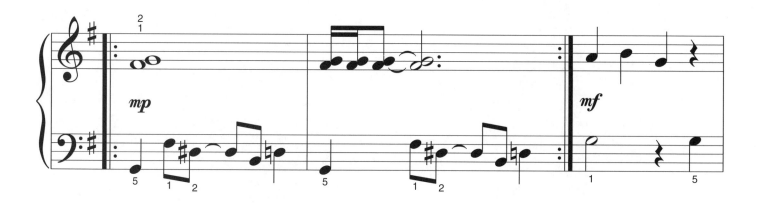

THEME FROM E.T.
(The Extra-Terrestrial)
from the Universal Picture E.T. (THE EXTRA-TERRESTRIAL)

Music by JOHN WILLIAMS

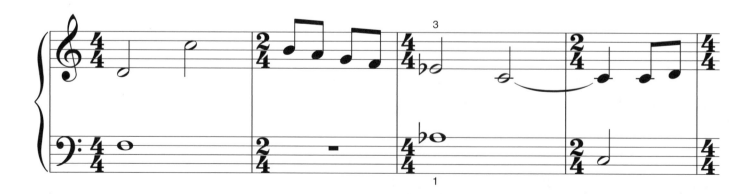

5

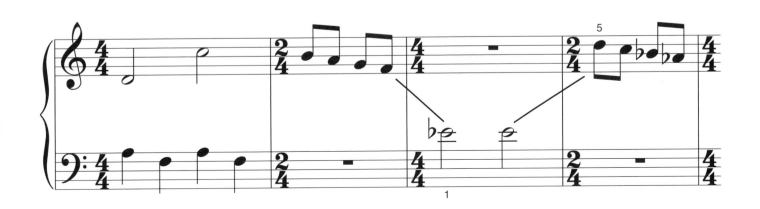

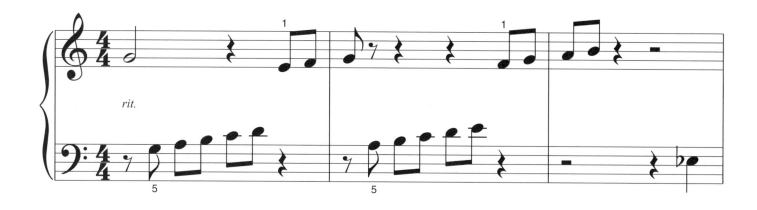

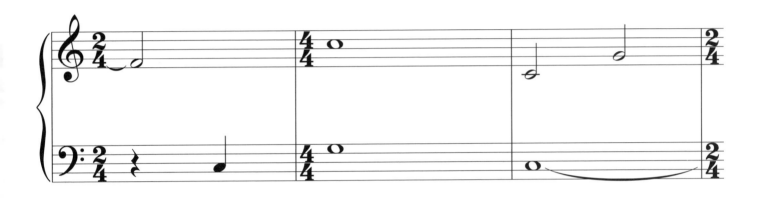

HARRY'S WONDROUS WORLD

from HARRY POTTER AND THE SORCERER'S STONE

By JOHN WILLIAMS

Moderately

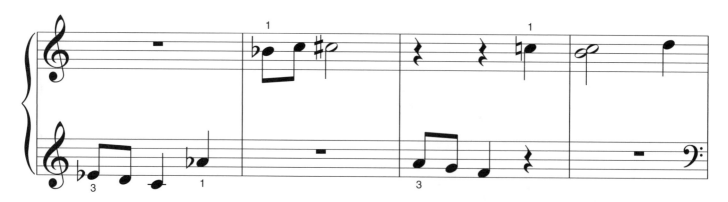

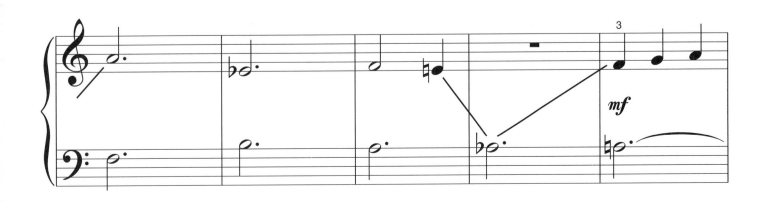

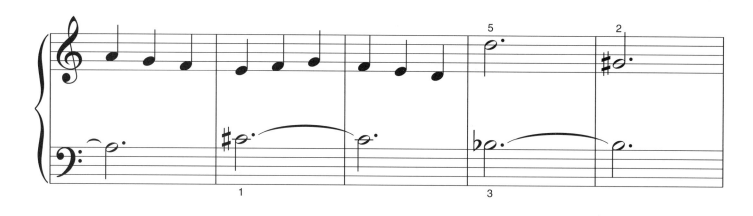

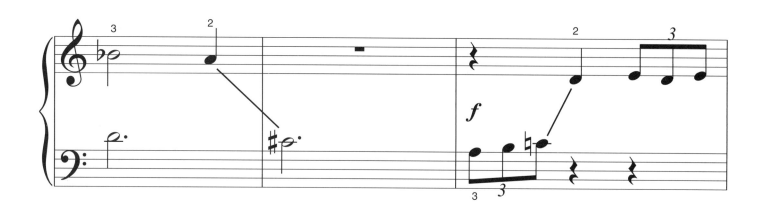

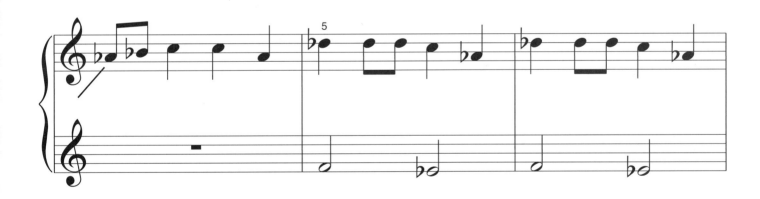

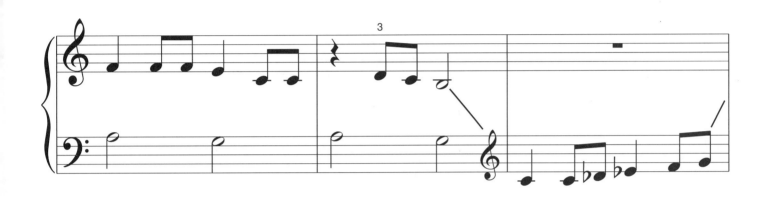

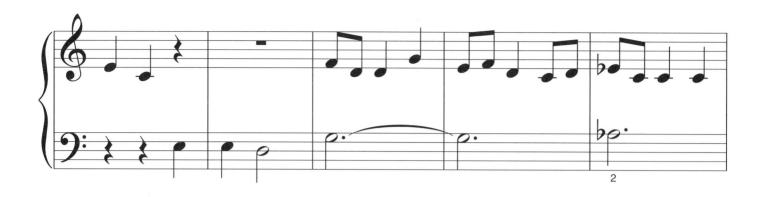

THE HOMECOMING

from the Motion Picture WAR HORSE

Composed by
JOHN WILLIAMS

Moderately fast, in 2

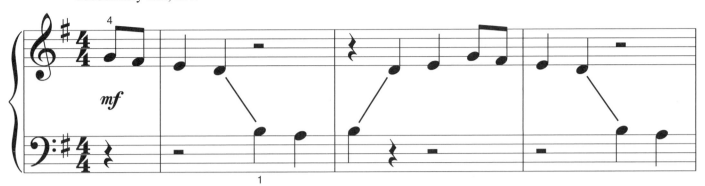

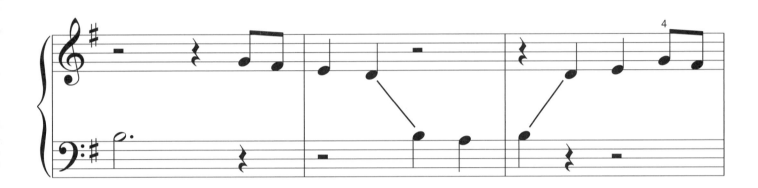

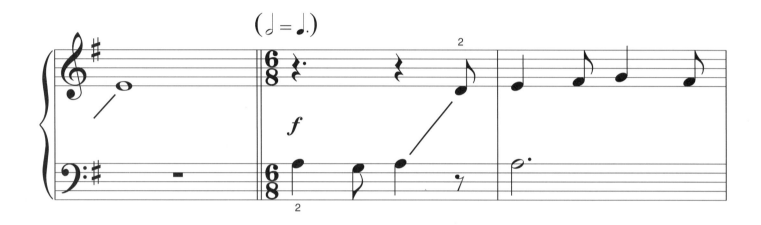

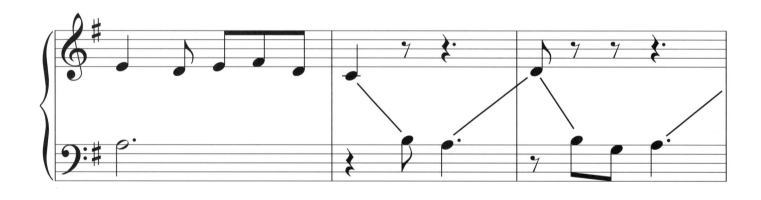

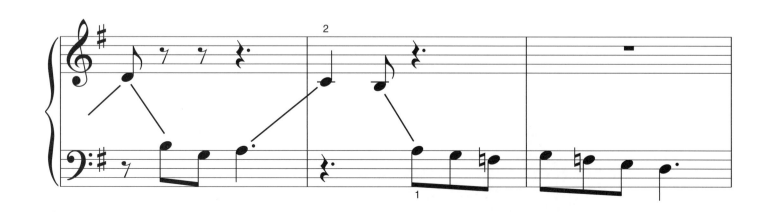

Slowly, with freedom

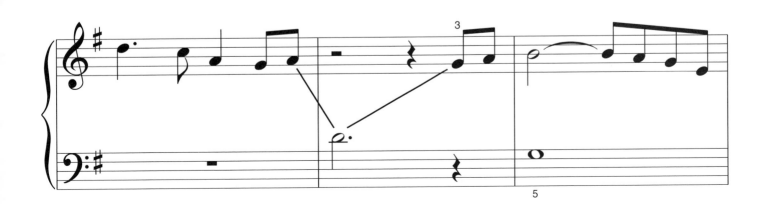

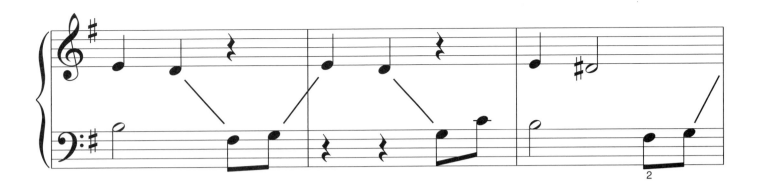

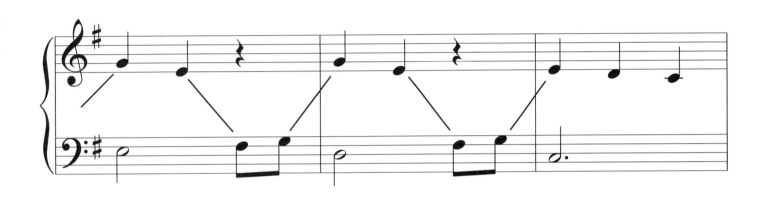

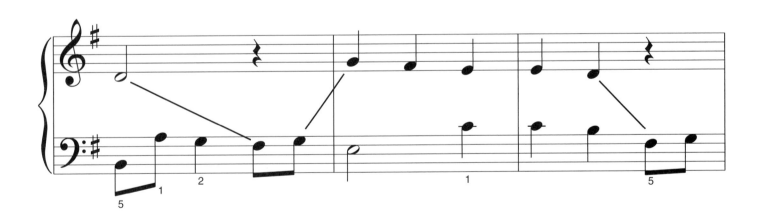

HYMN TO THE FALLEN

from the Paramount and DreamWorks Motion Picture SAVING PRIVATE RYAN

Music by
JOHN WILLIAMS

Slowly, reverently

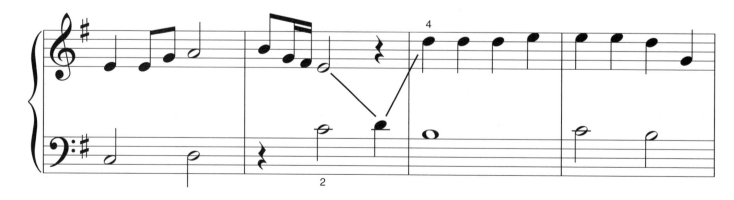

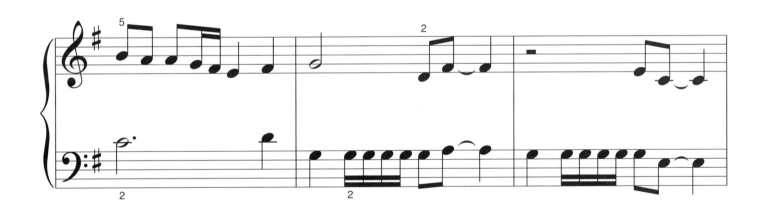

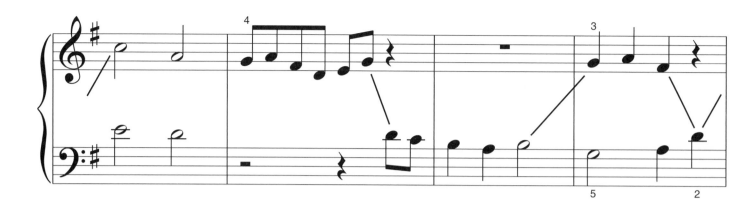

THEME FROM "JAWS"

from the Universal Picture JAWS

By JOHN WILLIAMS

Very steady and threatening

LH 8vb throughout

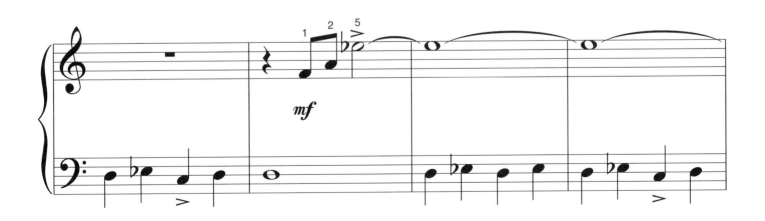

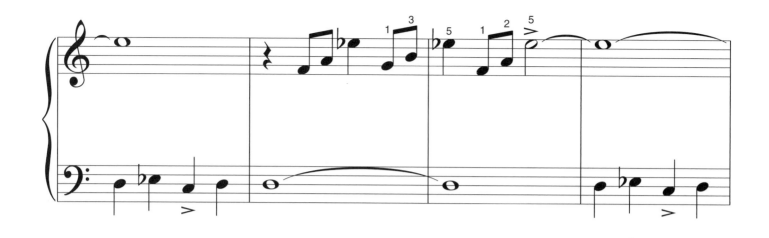

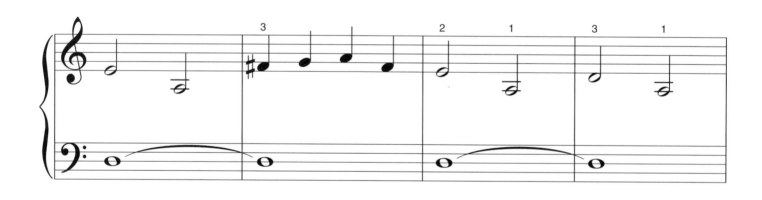

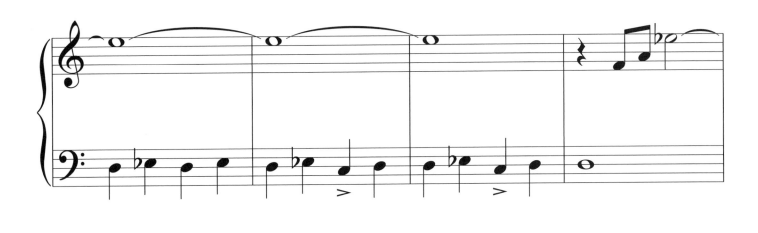

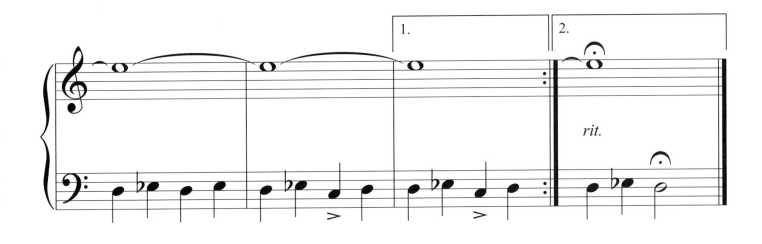

THE IMPERIAL MARCH
(Darth Vader's Theme)
from STAR WARS: THE EMPIRE STRIKES BACK

Music by
JOHN WILLIAMS

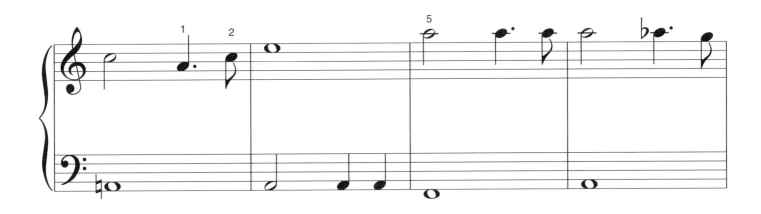

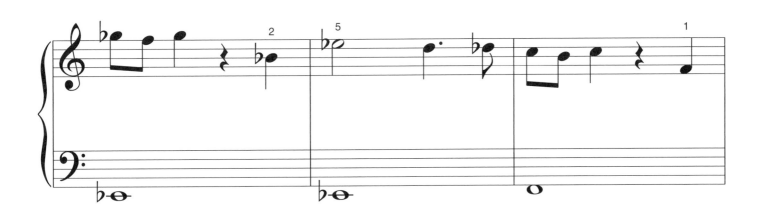

THEME FROM "JURASSIC PARK"

from the Universal Motion Picture JURASSIC PARK

Composed by
JOHN WILLIAMS

MARCH OF THE RESISTANCE

from STAR WARS: THE FORCE AWAKENS

Music by
JOHN WILLIAMS

Crisply

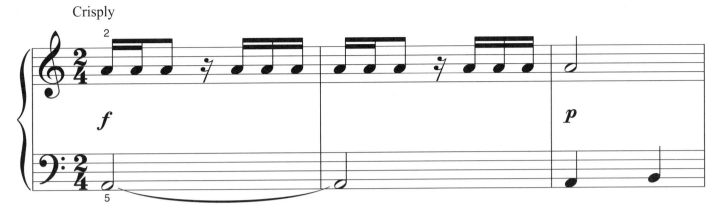

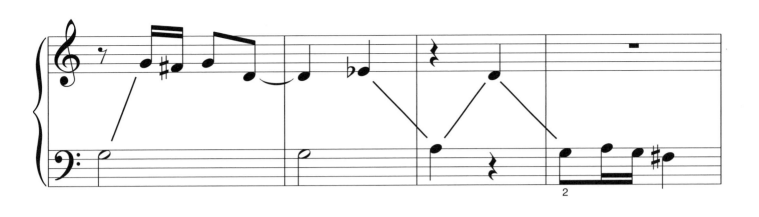

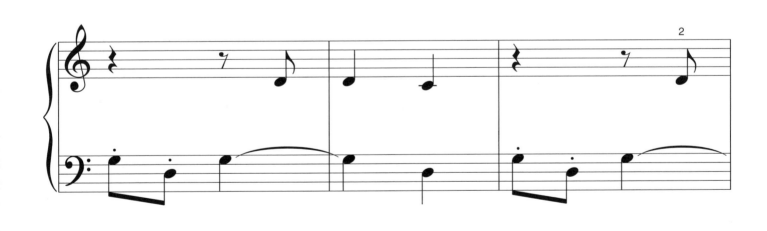

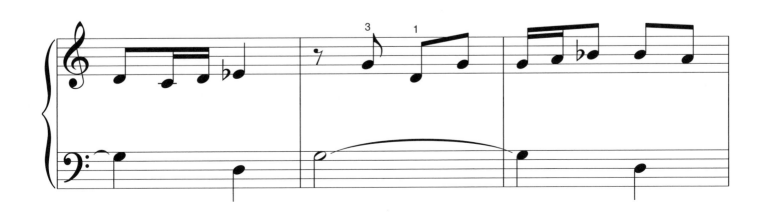

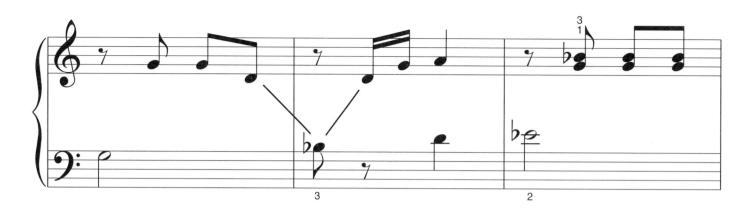

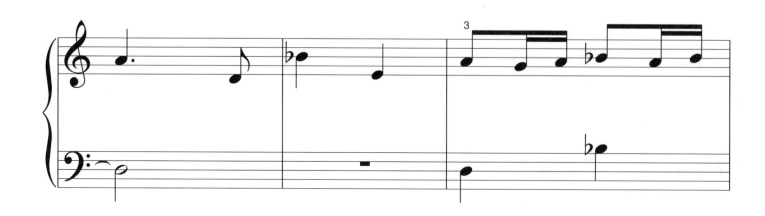

RAIDERS MARCH
from the Paramount Motion Picture RAIDERS OF THE LOST ARK

Music by
JOHN WILLIAMS

Steady March

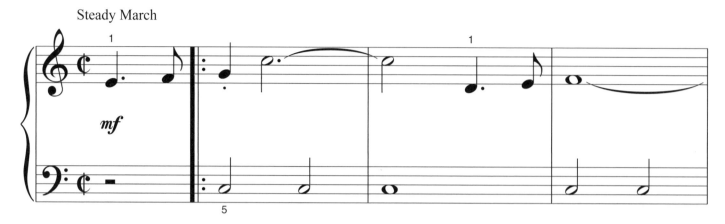

REY'S THEME
from STAR WARS: THE FORCE AWAKENS

Music by
JOHN WILLIAMS

Moderately, steadily

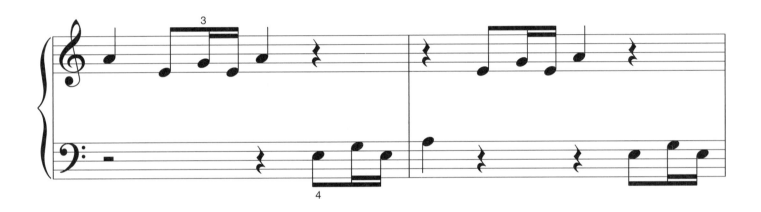

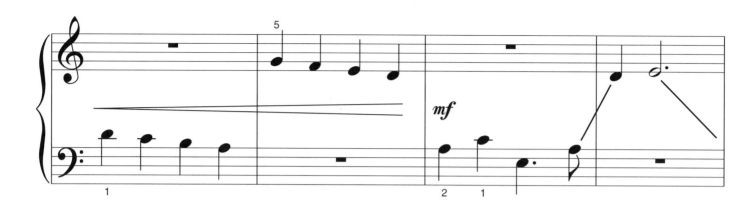

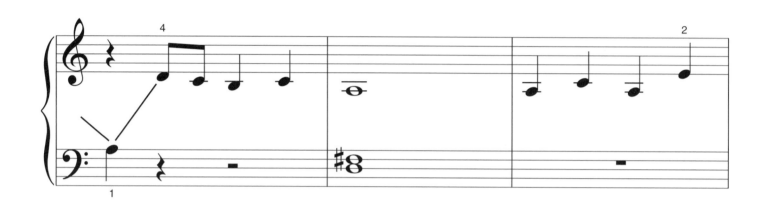

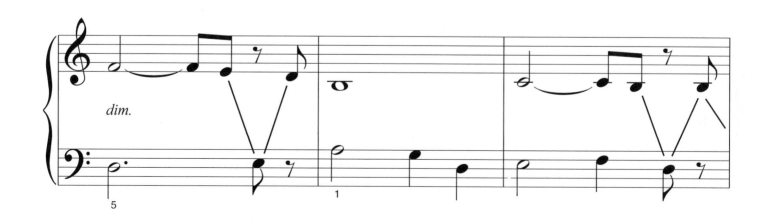

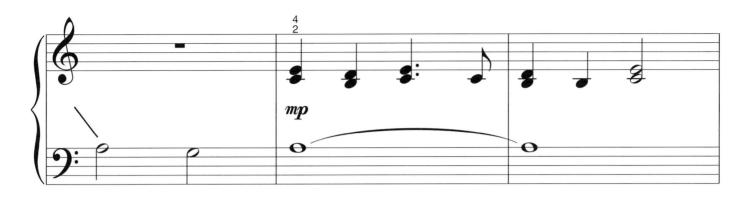

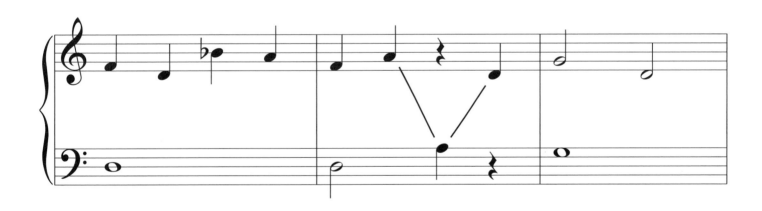

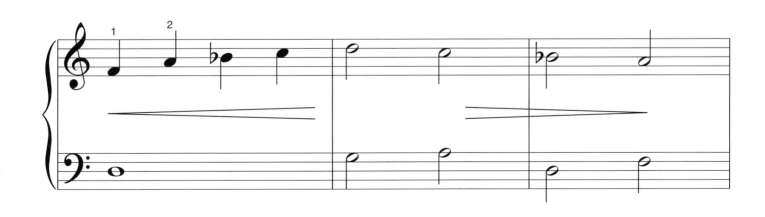

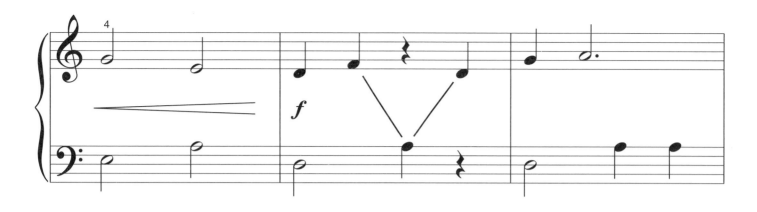

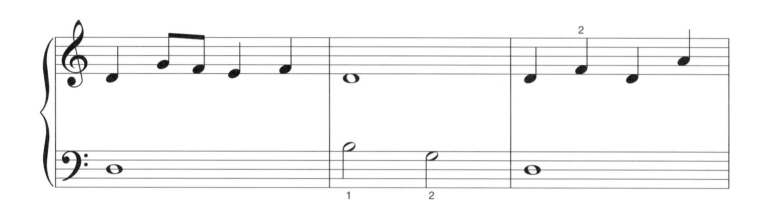

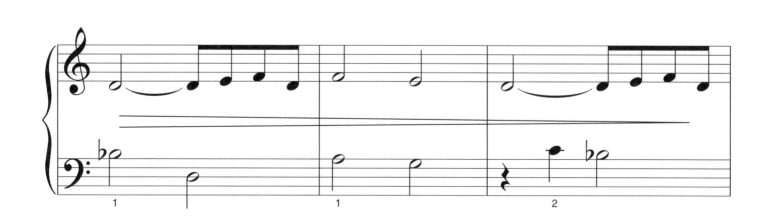

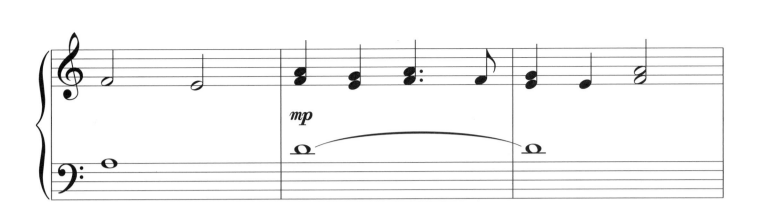

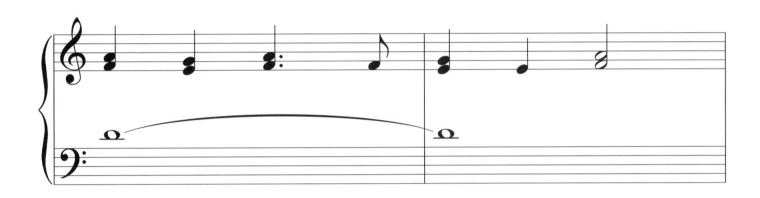

THEME FROM "SCHINDLER'S LIST"

from the Universal Motion Picture SCHINDLER'S LIST

Music by
JOHN WILLIAMS

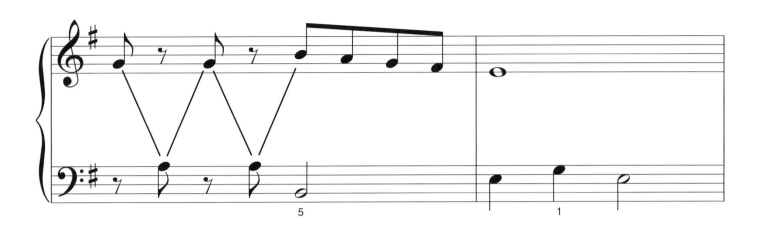

D.S. al Coda

CODA

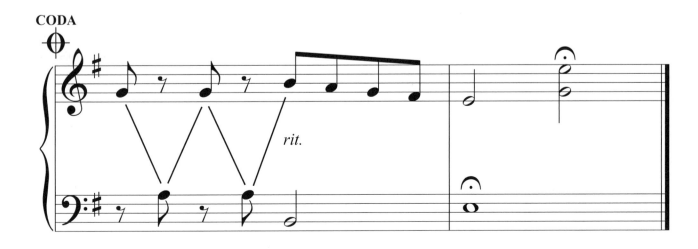

STAR WARS
(Main Theme)
from STAR WARS: A NEW HOPE

Music by
JOHN WILLIAMS

Majestically

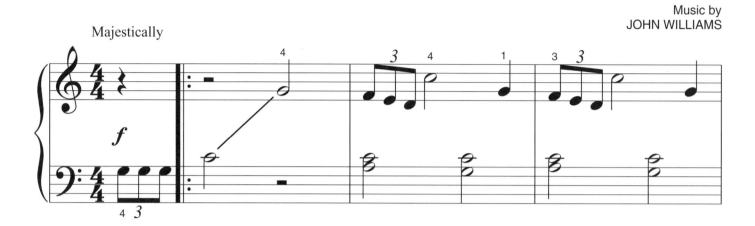

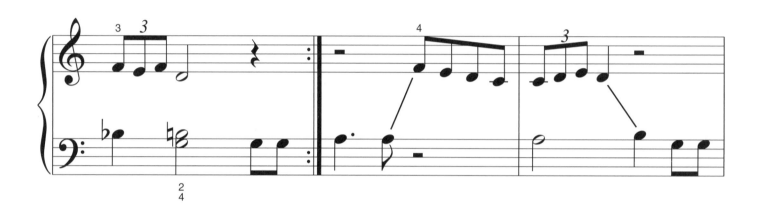

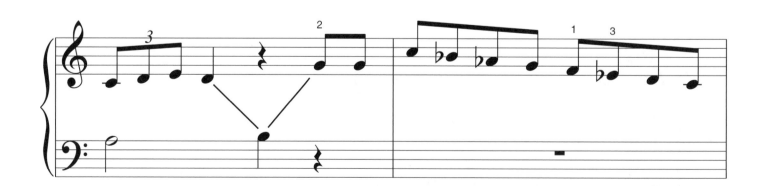

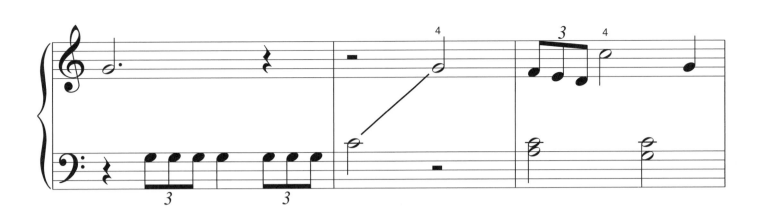

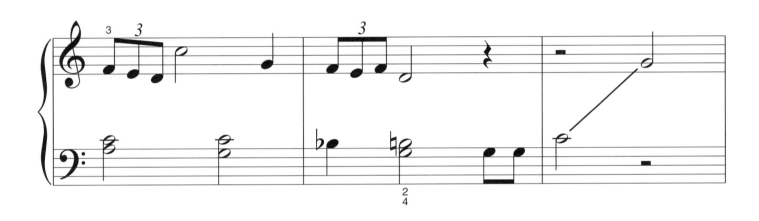

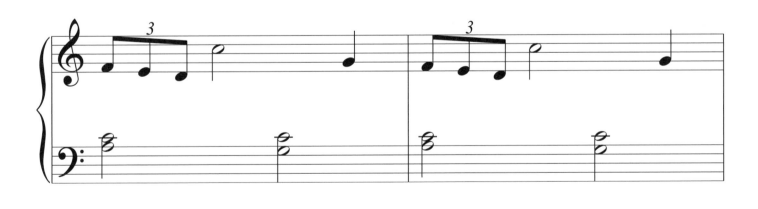

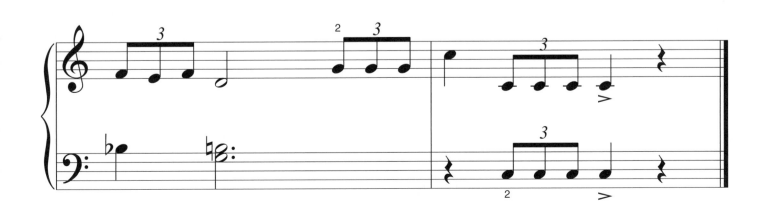

SOPHIE'S THEME

from THE BFG

By JOHN WILLIAMS

Slowly, with innocence

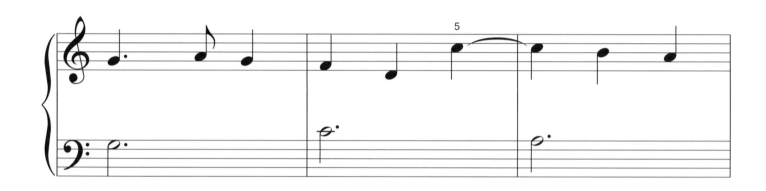

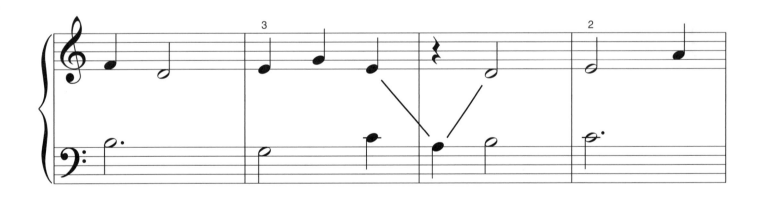

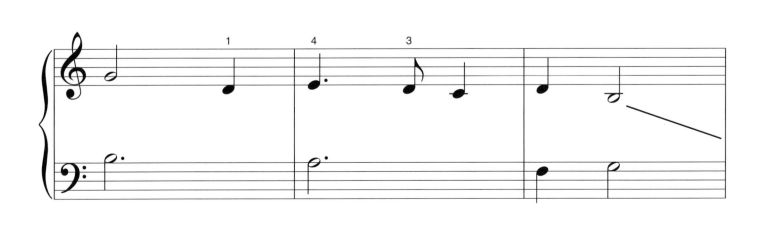

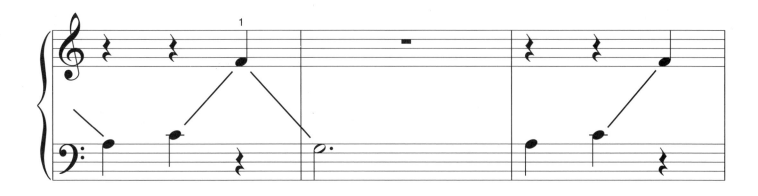

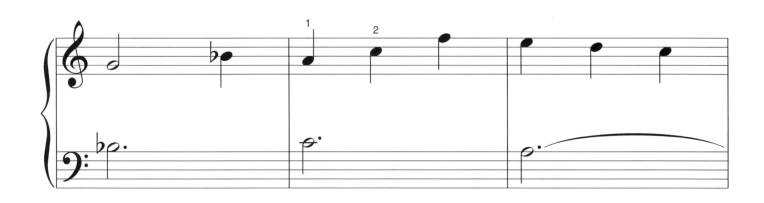

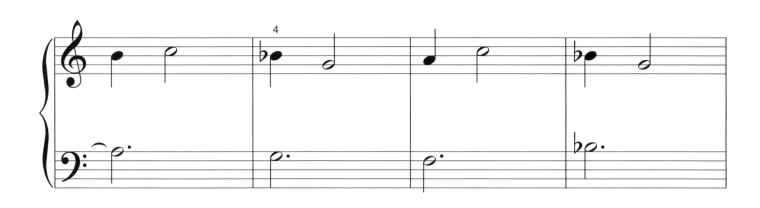

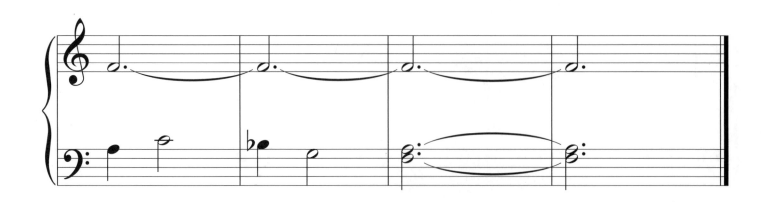